# YOSEMITE

❧ 1872 ❧

**≼ 1872 ≽**

# YOSEMITE

## THE YOSEMITE FALLS

Written and Illustrated
By James D. Smillie

Applewood Books

CARLISLE, MASSACHUSETTS

# PUBLISHER'S NOTE

In November 1870, Picturesque America was launched by American publisher Appleton & Co. as a "series of papers…consisting of splendidly-executed views of the most unfamiliar and novel features of American scenery." Over the next four years, nine hundred images and hundreds of thousands of words were sent out, by subscription, to a large audience. It was one of the first printed publications to celebrate an American nationalism based in the physical world rather than in the political or historical realm. Utilizing all of the modern methods of printing and distribution of the day, Picturesque America beautifully instructed Americans how to think about their country. Physically and emotionally torn by the Civil War, America of the 1870s needed healing. Picturesque America gave to Americans a way to envision the seemingly unchanging landscape of the country at a time that celebrated advancement, science, and discovery.

We are today a bit wary of progress and the ways that we use our precious land. We are concerned about climate. We see landscape as something humans have the power to destroy or to protect. We look backward and see simpler days. The handmade books that we are publishing as part of our Picturesque America series are made from the images and words of hope sent out over a century and a half ago. Our America is different—today, we celebrate and preserve what is beautiful and needing of our protection.

—Applewood Books

# THE YOSEMITE FALLS.

Half-Dome, from the Merced River.

THE journey from the Atlantic to the Pacific is a fitting introduction to the Yosemite, which most nobly crowns the grandest pleasure-tour within the limits of our country. Palace, drawing-room, sleeping, and hotel cars, do not suggest, in title at least, the weariness of travel; and the vast country traversed presents so great a variety of interest that all sense of monotony is banished, as, day after day and night after night, the sleepless engine rushes on, tireless.

Two days and a half, flying at railroad speed through
fleeting landscape, with now and then a busy town or
great, roaring city—two nights of hurrying sleep, and
the journey from the Atlantic to the Missouri River
is complete. The great plains of North America
stretch away to the west, seemingly boundless as the
ocean; a wild spirit of freedom breathes in the very
air that pipes and whistles through the train, in true
nautical style, as the third night folds its dark curtains
over these limitless wilds, and the sun of the fourth
morning rises upon the same unbroken scene. Then
come grand views of the distant Rocky Mountains,
followed by the wonder-land of the Green-River
country, where cliffs tower, wild and fantastic in
form and color. Farther on, the grim walls of Echo,
Weber, Devil's Gate, and Ogden Cañons, echo and
reëcho the roar and thunder of the intruding train.
The Wahsatch Mountains are passed, and the heavy
waters of Salt Lake ripple and blaze, like burnished
gold, in the light of the setting sun. On the morrow,
barren, treeless mountains, alkali-desert, and sage-
brush, reign supreme. Daybreak of the seventh, and
last morning, gladdens the eyes with a sight of sturdy
evergreen-forests. Now there is but a long downhill to
the plains of California; the character of the forest-
growth changes; herbage is scant, and the bare earth is
red-brown ; the air is hot, and has lost the exhilarating
vitality of the morning, heat trembles over the plain,
and soon the engine pants in the seething crowd at
Sacramento. Once more under way, the barriers of

successive folds of the Coast Range are passed; and, at the close of day, crossing the bay to San Francisco, the chill Pacific wind greets the Atlantic traveller, forcing him, with a shiver, to draw close the overcoat that at noon would have been insufferable.

The Yosemite Valley lies among the Sierra Nevadas of California, nearly in the centre of the State, north and south, and midway between the east and west bases of the mountains, at this point a little over seventy miles wide. In a direct line it is one hundred and fifty miles almost due east from San Francisco, but at present it can hardly be reached by less than two hundred and fifty miles of travel. The name is an Anglicized or corrupted form of the Indian A-hom-e-tae, which means Great Grizzly Bear, supposed to be the title of a chief, and applied generally to a tribe that held possession of the region from the valley to the plains on the west. That name, however, was never given it by the Indians. They call it A-wah-nee, which finds its equivalent in the Spanish cañon or the English chasm.

In 1851 the miners and early settlers on the Mariposa estate were driven to desperation by these thieving Indians. A military company was organized to operate against them, and, directed by Tenaya, a friendly red-skin, they followed the flying and astonished aborigines into their innermost hiding-place, the now famous Yosemite. It was then the turn of the white men to be astonished; and, when the company returned to the settlements, marvellous

Big Trees—Mariposa Grove.

stories were told of what had been seen. This is the story of the discovery. The Indians did not lay their first lesson well to heart. They continued their depredations, and, in consequence, another expedition chased them from their stronghold the following year. They fled to the protection of a powerful tribe, the Monos, farther in among the mountains; were hospitably received by them, but betrayed their confidence, and, in return, were slaughtered almost to the last man. Reports vary, but it is generally agreed that less than half a dozen of the Yosemite tribe now survive.

It was not until 1855 that the first tourists' visit was made to the valley. Then a party went in, under the guidance of Mr. J. M. Hutchings. The same season a second party followed; next year a trail was completed on the Mariposa side, and regular pleasure-travel commenced. The same year (1856) the first house or shanty was put up; but to Mr. J. C. Lamon belongs the credit of being the first actual settler. He built a cabin, and yet lives there, alone, summer and winter.

In 1864 Congress passed an act fixing the boundaries, and setting apart, "for public use, resort, and recreation," the Yosemite Valley and the Mariposa Grove of Big Trees. The State of California was to appoint commissioners and assume the trust, which at once she did, and the people of the United States rejoiced in their grand park. Claims have been made based upon the rights of settlers to land in the valley, but the courts have decided adversely to them.

It was one morning in June, as bright as such mornings usually are, that our little party started for Yosemite. Taking cars on the Central Pacific Railroad, we returned east eighty miles to Lathrop, and then, on what is known as the Visalia Division, turned south, crossing diagonally the broad valley of the San Joaquin. The road is now finished, so that travellers may go almost to the foot-hills of the Sierras by rail. We trundled along in good old style, with a coach-and-six. The wheat-harvest was already being gathered, and nothing could be more foreign to Eastern eyes than the huge machinery, barn-like in dimensions, drawn by a score of mules, "heading" a swathe of at least fifteen feet wide. Every thing was in. proportion to the vast fields, of thousands of acres each, that had to be worked over. The heads only of the wheat were cut off, the stalks being left for fertilization, or for the cattle that are allowed to range, fall and winter, over these fenceless plains. The exact line of our road seemed to be largely a matter of will on the part of our driver, for he drove wherever he pleased; no barriers prevented, and most of the grain had been cut. No tree, or bush, or living green thing, gave vitality to the landscape. Through a thin, tremulous haze, the forms of the Sierras in the east, and the Coast Range in the west, were faintly visible. The sky overhead was cloudless, a deep violet tint pervading, in strong contrast to the earth-tones of ochre and orange—a strange combination, blending duskily at the horizon, and in tint and tone calling to mind familiar pictures of Egypt, Syria, and the East. After several hours' riding, exposed to a fierce sun, the scene became monotonous, and by degrees very tiresome.

At last the Sierra forms loomed up, distinct and near, inviting visions of breezy heights and refreshing forest shadows; but hours of disappointment followed, for, to the toil of climbing among the foot-hills, was added the loss of the breeze that blows regularly over the plains, even though it were a warm one. Already, at this season, the earth was browned; herbage was scant; ochre, umber, and sienna-tints prevailed; the leaves of the buckeye were falling, crisp and dry; dust covered the glossy green of the beautiful manzanita; the digger-pines stood samples of attenuation; and, over all, pervading all, was a sentiment not so much of decay as desiccation. Hornitas, an irregular and uninteresting gathering of buildings, was passed; and, from the heights beyond, the plains could be seen stretching in luminous obscurity. Very gradually the barrenness gave place to chaparrals of oak, manzanita, and chamiso; and trees clothed the crests of the mountain-spurs, after the manner of forests. At last we reached Mariposa, about thirty miles from the plains by the road we travelled, and calling to memory only a dusty, hot street; low, shabby-looking brick buildings; and surrounding hills, that were without any compensating wildness or beauty to excuse them for standing as barriers to the longed-for breezes. Here the forests began to assume a more familiar appearance, as oaks and evergreens clustered in denser growth. Ten or fifteen miles farther on, at an elevation of more than three thousand feet, the timber was superb. Coniferous trees preponderated, different varieties of oak being next in importance. Compared with Eastern-State forests, there is very little undergrowth, the woods having a singularly open appearance, and showing to great advantage the noble sugar- and pitch-pines, many of which are more than two hundred feet high, and from seven to ten feet in diameter. It might be fancied that, in forests where trees attained such proportions, there would be majestic solemnity, sylvan recesses, depths profound, and what not. On the contrary, an air of cheerfulness reigned, as the sunshine, streaming through, lighted into bright, warm color the shaft-like trunks of pitch-pine and cedar. At Clark's Ranch,

Fallen Sequoia.

more than fifty miles from the plains, the carriage-road ends, but it has been surveyed and partially completed into the Yosemite. Here, then, the scant baggage was to be transferred to the backs of mules, and the remaining twenty-four miles done in the saddle; but, before going on, it is usual to spend a day among the big trees of Mariposa, four miles distant, but not in the direction of the Yosemite.

Bridal-Veil Fall.

The grant of the Mariposa Grove covers four sections, or two miles square, and is under the charge of the Yosemite commissioners. The first that was known of the big trees was in the spring of 1852, when a hunter discovered what is now called the Calaveras Grove. He could get no one to believe his story, and had to resort to a trick to get any of his companions to go with him to the trees, so as to verify his statements. Once verified, descriptions were widely published, and, from San Francisco papers, copied into English prints. In 1853 an English botanist published a scientific description, and designated the tree as the *Wellingtonia gigantea*. In 1854 an eminent French botanist, M. Decaisne, at a meeting of the "Société Botanique de France," presented specimens of the big trees and redwood that he had received from the consular agent of France at San Francisco. He explained at length his reasons for considering the big tree and redwood as belonging to the same species, *Sequoia*, an affinity the English botanist had overlooked; so, in accordance with the rules of botanical nomenclature, the new species was called *Sequoia gigantea*. Professor Whitney, State Geologist of California (upon whose faithful work I have drawn liberally), says: "It is to the happy accident of the generic agreement of the big tree with the redwood that we owe it that we are not obliged to call the largest and most interesting tree of America after an English military hero. Had it been an English botanist of the highest eminence, the dose would not have been so unpalatable." (Sequoia, it will be remembered, was the name of the Cherokee Indian who, early in this century, invented an alphabet and written language for his tribe.) So far as is yet known, there are but eight distinct patches or groves of the big trees. They are very lmited in range, and seem to belong exclusively to California. They form groves, largely intermixed with other trees, very little below five thousand and never over seven thousand feet above sea-level. They have been, without difficulty, largely propagated from the seed, and fine specimens are now growing in many parts of America and Europe. A few miles south of the Mariposa Grove, the *Sequoias* seem to find a more congenial home, and may be found of all ages and sizes, from the seedling up. A mill, at this place, saws them into lumber. Professor Whitney closes his very interesting chapter by saying: "The big tree is not that wonderfully exceptional thing which popular writers have almost always described it as being. It is not so restricted in its range as some other coniferæ of California. It occurs in great abundance, of all ages and sizes, and there is no reason to suppose that it is now dying out, or that it belongs to a past geological era, any more than the redwood.

"The age of the big trees is not so great as that assigned by the highest authorities to some of the English yews. Neither is its height as great, by far, as that of an Australian species, the *Eucalyptus amygdalina*, many of which have, on the authority of Dr. Müller, the eminent government botanist, been found to measure over four hundred feet." The tallest *Sequoia* that has been measured is in the Calaveras Grove, being three hundred and twenty-five feet high, overtopping Trinity-Church spire (a standard of height familiar to most New-Yorkers) by forty feet. The greatest in diameter is the "Grizzly Giant" in the Mariposa Grove, which measures thirty-one feet through at the ground, and twenty feet at eleven feet above the ground. Clarence King described one that he saw in the forest some miles south of Mariposa, "a slowly-tapering, regularly round column, of about forty feet in diameter at the base, and rising two hundred and seventy-four feet." A very large tree in the Calaveras Grove, twenty-four feet in diameter, was, after much labor, cut down, and the base, at six feet from the ground, was smoothed and prepared as a dancing-floor; thirty feet farther up, the trunk was again cut through, and the rings, marking the growth of each year, were carefully counted. Upon this evidence, after making allowances and calculations, Professor Torrey pronounced the tree about thirteen hundred years old. It is not likely that any now standing are much older.

The ride from Clark's Ranch to the grove is less than four miles; so, after an early breakfast, we started for a day of picnic and sketching. The trail was well worn and easy, the air gloriously pure, and the forest delightful. It would be useless to attempt to describe the confusion of sentiment and impatience that possessed me as I rode along, peering anxiously through the labyrinth of the wood for the first glimpse into the vast portals of that grand old grove. Memory recalled the solemn gloom of a hemlock-forest among the Catskill Mountains—if that was dark, then surely this must be savage—if that was solemn, then this must be awful! To me, the sighing of summer breezes through those high tops would be the ghostly echo of wild storms that had done battle with them for hundreds of years. Inarticulate with the lore of dead ages, their moans would breathe the sad history of centuries past; their towering heads, with scarce perceptible nod, would tell of Goths and Vandals that scourged Europe when they were young; of King Arthur and "his table round," while yet they were in the vigor of early maturity; and of Mohammed and his wars, written upon the page of history, before their limbs creaked with age. They might whisper something of lost races on this continent, or of the advent of the red-man; to them Columbus would be a matter of yesterday, and our dear Revolutionary

Valley Floor, with View of Cathedral Spires.

War a scarce noticeable thing of to-day. The guide shouts, "There is a big tree!" What! are we so near the sacred precincts? Where is the atmosphere of awe? where the elements that were to hush the voice, and fill the whole being with reverential exaltation? Alas! there was the first big tree, sunlight sparkling all over its great cinnamon-colored trunk, and I was ready to shout, and, spurring my prosaic beast, to rush with the rest in a graceless scramble to be first to reach his majesty's foot. The charm was broken. I was willing, anxious to be deeply moved, but no answering emotion came—such moods do not come at the bidding. Unsought, they have welled up since at thought of that day—but not then; no, not then. I had built an ideal grove, and at first sight it was demolished, but that was no fault of the Mariposa big trees. There was no gloomily grand grove, there were no profound recesses; the great trees stood widely apart, with many pines and firs interspersed, and sunlight streamed down through all and over all. I wandered about, sorely disappointed that they did not look bigger, and yet every sense told me that they were vast beyond any thing that I had ever seen; and it was not until after I had been among them for hours, and had sketched two or three, that their true proportions loomed upon my understanding. Then I wondered at the practical man who was "pacing-off" the diameter of the "Grizzly Giant," and at the woman of little faith, who had brought with her a piece of twine to verify the oft-told story of size. It is hardly possible to form a just idea of size or height until, getting at a distance where the whole tree may be seen, a mounted figure takes position at the base, thus establishing an initial point for computation. In form they are often savagely gaunt, their respiratory apparatus of foliage being in remarkably small proportion to their tower-like trunks. The bark is very light and fibrous, like the outer sheath of a cocoa-nut, of a singular cinnamon-color, and running in great ridges that vary from ten inches to three feet in thickness. Some trunks appear quite smooth, but others are warted and gnarled as though wearing the wrinkles of great age. The Indians and sheep-herders have been accustomed every year to burn the undergrowth through the woods, and by this practice, now strictly prohibited, most of the trees in the Mariposa Grove have been injured, a few but slightly; but, in many cases, soundness and beauty have been seriously impaired. On an area of thirty-seven hundred by twenty-three hundred feet there are just three hundred and sixty-five *Sequoias* of a diameter of one foot or over, but not more than twenty are over twenty feet in diameter. Two or three, greater than any that stand, now lie prone and broken; the trail lies through the hollow section of one that has fallen and been burned out. An ordinary-sized man, sitting upon a horse, can but just touch with his knuckles the blackened arch overhead.

The afternoon, rich in contrasts of glowing lights and broad shadows, too quickly followed the

Cathedral Spires.

inquisitive glare of noonday sun; pictures in effect and color presented themselves where, an hour before, there had been only a confusion of petty forms, sharp and shadowless, under the almost perpendicular rays of sunlight; the novelty of first acquaintance was wearing off, and the true grandeur of proportions was developing with fascinating rapidity. The spirit was groaning within me that pencil and color in my hands were so weak, when through the hush came the faintest mutterings of distant thunder. The rest of the party had gone, and with them the picnic element. I was alone, and the booming of the rapidly-nearing storm, as its echoing waves of sound rolled through the pillared forest that seemed to stand dumbly expectant, was to me the grand original, of which grimly-solemn cathedral and deepest organ-note are but a type. Threatening clouds darkened the sky, a few great drops of rain adding emphasis to the warning. Hastily gathering my scattered scraps, I retreated, but not without a last, hungry, devouring look. Now there is pictured in memory a mighty shadowed forest, its branches moving uneasily, and sighing as the storm sweeps torrent-like through it.

As has been already stated, Clark's Ranch is the present end of the carriage-road, and the beginning of the bridle-path into the Yosemite, which is only twelve miles distant in a direct line, although nearly twice that by the trail. Its altitude is about four thousand feet, being a little higher than the floor of the valley, but between it and the valley lies an elevation that must be crossed, which is about three thousand five hundred feet in height, nearly equal to the average of the Catskill Mountains, the highest point reached in crossing being seven thousand four hundred feet above the sea. Here are barns and stables, a saw-mill, and several long, low, irregular one-story houses, with characteristic arrangement of verandas, upon which open all the doors and windows, there being no passages or hall-ways in the buildings. Guides, hunters, and dogs, loiter about; horses wait in groups, saddled and bridled; uneasy travellers flit from house to house, and an air of business generally possesses the place, in spite of the close, hedging, heavy timber, that brings the air of the primeval wilderness to the very doors.

Our scant luggage was securely packed for the ride, and early in the morning the horses were brought out—a dejected-looking lot, each with a rope-halter about its neck, giving more the appearance of so many candidates for the gallows than toilers for a pleasure-party. It was interesting to watch the packing of the load upon the mule's back, the curiously-intricate cording and strapping, and then the final binding of beast and burden into one inseparable mass. Two strong men laid hold of the ropes, the passive mule between them, and pulled as though striving each to outdo the other. Could toughened hide or bony framework resist? The brute made no sign. They placed each a foot against the pack, and their weight was added to their muscle for one final effort; a faint ugh! came from the stolid creature, and a crunching sound, as of a great eggshell in collapse, told me that my sketch-box had come to grief; but no matter, there was no time to stop for trifles; a heavy hand took hold upon the top of the pack, vigorously shook it—the mule vibrated as though it were part and parcel. "He must get out of his skin before he can get out of that," said the guide, and he was started on the trail.

Sentinel Rock and Fall.

It is not necessary to go all the way to the Yosemite to enjoy the picturesque effects of a party of pleasure-seekers, en route. The gay colors that inevitably find

Sentinel Rock from the North.

place, the grouping, action, light and shade in constantly-changing combination with the surrounding landscape, are a never-failing source of pleasure. Now, in bright sunlight, every spot of color tells with intensest power against a mass of sombre green; again, in the deep shadow of a wood, they form yet deeper shadows, and their richer color darkens against the light beyond. Crossing an open space, how a white horse with red-shirted rider puts a climax upon all that there is of light and color; or, straggling over an upland waste of blinding-white granite-sand, how invaluable to the picture the strong relief of the black mule and his grotesque pack! So we spent the morning, crossing streams and climbing hill-sides, thankful for the cool, fragrant shadow of dark pines, and rejoicing in the light of broad meadows brilliant with flowers, and opening into long vistas hedged with close-standing fir-trees. Now and then a broad waste of rock had to be passed, and several times, from heights, we had views of the high Sierra peaks. It was soon after noon when we reached Paregoy's, a cattle-ranch and half-way house. Meadows, covered with natural grasses, following the course of running streams, stretched for miles in narrow belts, where great numbers of horses and cattle roamed and found pasture. We were surprised by a remarkably good dinner, although the request for a boiled egg could not be complied with—twenty minutes of trying proved an utter failure; we were a little over seven thousand feet "up in the world," where eggs do not observe the "three and a half minute" rule as they do upon lower levels. It was not long before we were again mounted and on the way, impatient to get over the five miles that intervened between us and Inspiration Point. If, the day before, we rode in the excitement of expectation, it was intensified now; every step brought us nearer to a place that hitherto had been to me like some crater in the moon or spot on the sun. There was no doubt as to its existence, but it belonged to the realm of fancy, now to be transferred to the real—a change almost dreaded. It is dangerous work to force our ideals from fancy to fact from poetry to prose. I knew it, and these questions were constantly repeated: Was grim disappointment waiting? were the senses to be benumbed on that dizzy height? would every line and every color harmonize to produce an effect overwhelming? At last, through the trees, there gleamed a pale, mist-like whiteness—it must be a wall of rock—could that be the first sight into the valley? The pulse quickened, the hard saddle and the shabby shamble of the offending beast underneath were forgotten, as he forced himself into quicker gait in answer to impatient drubbings; a few moments more, and we rode out to a clear space under pine-trees, where every evidence was presented of the many feet that had halted there before us; so, following their indications, and the

Rock Slide.

unmistakable suggestions of our prosaic beasts, we alighted, and fastened them to well-worn branches of pine or manzanita. A few yards only of *chaparral* intervened between us and the cliff—a rush and a bound—in a moment our feet were upon Inspiration Point, and—Mr. Clarence King, for whose descriptive powers I have great admiration, says: "I always go swiftly by this famous point of view now, feeling somehow that I don't belong to that army of literary travellers who have here planted themselves and burst into rhetoric. Here all who make California books, down to the last and most sentimental specimen who so much as meditates a letter to his or her local paper, dismount and inflate."

Warned by the lateness of the hour, and that we had yet seven miles to ride before we could reach the nearest house, we again mounted our horses, and commenced the descent, nearly three thousand feet in three miles, over a very tortuous trail, rocky or dusty by turns, extremely tiresome to the wearied body, but never dangerous, there being no cliffs or precipices such as formed the grand picture constantly before us. Pine-trees, more or less dense, sheltered the way; and the scenery was enough to lift any one, not hopelessly dead or unobservant, far above the petty discomforts of saddle or trail. Every change of position presented some new charm—trees grouped into picturesque foregrounds, finding bold relief in light and shade against the opal and amethyst tints of distant granite cliffs; flowers nodding in the breeze that brought refreshment to the brow and music to the ear; and little streams dimpling and gurgling across the trail, as if unconscious of the terrible leaps that must be taken before reaching the river below. In strong contrast to this living, moving beauty, beyond all, the walls, towers, and domes of the Yosemite rose grand, serene, impassive, broadly divided into tenderest shadow and sweetest sunlight, giving no impression of cold, implacable, unyielding granite, but of majesty, to which our hearts 'went out as readily as to the flowers and brooks at our feet. As we approached the level of the valley and the open meadows, the groves of trees and the winding river were more distinctly seen—the glorious, park-like character of the place presented itself. Why not cultivate carefully these natural beauties—make lawns of the meadows, trim out the woods that the different trees may develop their fullest form, and control the river's course with grass-grown banks? At last, the foot of the descent was reached, and away we cantered in the evening shades, the black-oaks lacing their branches overhead. Trees, bending in graceful framework, enclosed various pictures, one of the most charming being a view of the Bridal-veil Fall as it sprung over the wall nine hundred feet high. Its upper part sparkled a moment in the sunlight, a solid body; then, as though wrestling with invisible spirits, it swept into a wild swirl of spray that came eddying down in soft mists and formless showers. Emerging from the wood, a broad meadow lay before us; and high over all projected, far up against the eastern sky, the Cathedral Rocks, with buttresses cool and spires aglow. At their foot the river crowds so close that the trail is forced to find its way through a wilderness of great granite blocks, that lie embowered in a forest which has grown since they were hurled from their places on the cliffs above. Then followed a long level, and groves of pine and cedar. After the fatigue and excitement of the day, it was like entering a sanctuary, the spirit of the place was so solemn and full of rest. There was no sentiment of gloom, but rather of deep, slumberous repose; the thick carpeting of sienna-colored pine-spindles that covered the ground hushed each foot-fall; the pillared tree-trunks formed vistas that stretched, like "long-drawn aisles," to profoundest forest-depths; the branches, "intricately crossed," did not obscure the luminous sky above, or hide the tall cathedral-spires that burned ruddy in the last gleam of day; refreshment and invigoration were in the very atmosphere; with thankfulness, my whole being drank deeply, and, when in the gray of evening the hotel was reached, I was cool, calm, and—very hungry.

The first week after our arrival was spent making acquaintance with the more common points of interest and attraction. At first, submitting to the guides, we rode in beaten paths, and wondered and admired according to regulation; but, after a day or two, such bonds became irksome, and we ranged at will, there being really no need of a guide in an enclosure six miles long and at most but a mile and a half wide—no need of any one to direct attention to what the eyes could hardly fail to see, or the senses discover for themselves; and, then, it was so much more delightful to wander undirected and unattended, on horseback or on foot, regardless of conventional ways, and yielding unreservedly to each new enjoyment. We soon knew each meadow and the separating groves of trees, every stream and every ford across the river. Within the limits we ranged there are but eleven hundred and forty-one acres of level bottom, according to government reports—a surface only about one-third greater than that of the Central Park of New-York City—and of this seven hundred and forty-five acres are meadow, the rest being covered

Foot of Sentinel Fall.

with trees and *débris* of rock. From Tenaya Cañon, at
the upper end of the valley, to Bridal-veil Creek, near
the lower end, four and a half miles in a direct line,
the decline is only thirty-five feet. Naturally enough,
a surface so nearly level is very widely overflowed
during the high water in the spring, caused by
melting snows among the mountains beyond. The
meadows are covered with coarse, scant grass;
and innumerable flowers, generally of exceeding
delicacy, find choicest beds in slight depressions,
where the water lies longest. Through these meadows
the Merced River winds from side to side, during
the summer an orderly stream, averaging, maybe,
seventy or eighty feet in width, the cold snow-water
shimmering in beautiful emerald greens as it flows
over the granite-sand of the bottom. Its banks are
fringed with alder, willow, poplar, cotton-wood, and
evergreens; upon the meadow-level are grouped, in
groves more or less dense, pines, cedars, and oaks, the
latter often bearing large growths of mistletoe; upon
the rock-talus, mingling with the pines and firs, the
live-oak is a distinctive feature; higher, and clinging in
crevices and to small patches of soil, the pungent bay
and evergreen oak form patches of verdure. From the
foot of Sentinel Fall an excellent view may be had
of the meadows, the groves, the river, and the slopes
at the foot of the walls of rock on either hand. On
the right is El Capitan, three thousand three hundred
feet high; on the left are the Cathedral Rocks, nearly
two thousand seven hundred feet in height—the two

forming what may be called the southern gate to the valley. Each of our illustrations, it is intended, shall present some characteristic feature of the valley. The opening cut was selected from many similar views at the upper end of the valley, where the pine-trees come down to the river's edge, and are mirrored in the still pools. Washington Column, more than two thousand feet high, stands out on the left, casting an afternoon shadow well up on the flank of the Half-dome, whose summit is almost five thousand feet above the river, or nine thousand feet above the sea. The distant view of the spires may serve to tell the story of the broad, tree-covered levels, so charming for scampers on horseback, and of the prisoning walls that are without suggestion of imprisonment. The spires are forms of splintered granite,

Yosemite Fall and Merced River.

about five hundred feet in height, and altogether not less than two thousand feet above the valley. Sentinel Rock combines more of picturesqueness and grandeur, perhaps, than any other rock-mass in the valley, its obelisk-like top reaching a height of over three thousand feet, the face-wall being almost vertical. The view from the north is taken from a point about midway between the foot of Yosemite Fall and Washington Column; the other is from a point as far south of it, presenting an entirely different aspect, its stupendous proportions dwarfing into littleness every thing at its base. The fall at the right, as shown in the illustration, exists only in the spring, as it depends entirely upon the melting snow for its supply. That its force and volume at times must be terrific, is evident from the gorge that it has hollowed at its foot. It is rarely that such exhibitions of destructive energy can be found. The climb up this water-torn gully ends all dreams of a well-ordered park below. Torrents pour into the valley as soon as the snow begins to melt, leaping the cliffs with indescribable fury, carrying immense rocks and great quantities of coarse granite-sand, to work destruction as they spread their burden over the level ground. In some places, this detritus has been deposited to the depth of several feet in a single spring. The air then is filled with the roaring of water-falls; the greater portion of the valley is overflowed; and the wayward Merced cuts for itself new channels, making wide waste in the change. At such times, the Yosemite Fall is described as grand beyond all power of expression. The summit of the upper fall is a little over two thousand six hundred feet above the valley; for fifteen hundred feet the descent is absolutely vertical, and the rock is like a wall of masonry. Before this, the fall of water sways and sweeps, yielding to the force of the fitful wind with a marvellous grace and endless variety of motion. For a moment it descends with continuous roar; in another instant it is caught, and, reversing its flight, rises upward in wreathing,

Indians making Chemuck.

eddying mists, finally fading out like a summer cloud. The full-page illustration is taken from a clump of pine-trees so near that, by the rapid foreshortening, the entire fall appears in very different proportions from those seen from the opposite side of the valley. Such a glimpse is given in the illustration "Indians bathing."

In the spring, water is an element of destruction,

in freezing as well as in thawing. The little rills that filter and percolate into every crack and crevice of rock by day, as they freeze at night, enable the frost to ply its giant leverage; and, when disaster from water seems to threaten every thing, there is added the shock of falling cliffs. The granite-walls are not homogeneous in structure, some portions being far less durable, under the action of time and the elements, than others. The Half-dome and El Capitan

Horse-Racing.

are magnificent masses, at whose feet the *débris* are comparatively slight; but that part known as the Union Rocks, between the Cathedral and Sentinel Rocks, has suffered very much from disintegration. Great cliffs have fallen, and avalanches of rock have ploughed their way down the slope to the bottom of the valley. While climbing in such surroundings, the wreck of some world is suggested, so vast the ruin and so pigmy the climber. No words can convey other than a feeble impression of the effects of mountains of granite, sharp and fresh in fracture, piled one upon the other, the torn fragments of a forest underneath, or strewed about, as though the greatest had been but as straws tossed in the wind. A broad track of desolation leads away up to the heights from which these rocks have been thrown.

The attention may be diverted from cliffs and torrents to the human element characteristic of the place, poor though that element be, and in the change find much that is interesting in the few Indians that straggle, vagrant and worthless, through the region. They seem to be without tribal organization, although they still have "pow-wows," where their leading men, conscious of the inevitable decay of the race, strive to reorganize them and arouse their dying spirit; but the red-men are now hopelessly debauched and demoralized. In general appearance, they are robust, and even inclined to be fleshy; this latter is accounted for by the fact that acorns, their staple of food, are extremely fattening. There were at times as many as fifty Indians of all descriptions, male and female, old and young, living in the valley in the most primitive fashion, their "wallies," or huts, consisting only of branches stuck into the earth in semicircular form, the leaf-covered boughs meeting overhead. Generally they are dirty and disagreeable; but their voices are sweet, and their language is really musical. That some Indians do wash, I have had ocular demonstration;

they are not all unqualifiedly dirty. While sitting at work on the river-bank, three young squaws came along and surprised me by deliberately preparing for a bath, not a hundred feet from me. They disported themselves with all the grace of mermaids, diving, swimming, and playing for nearly an hour in the cold snow-water. They stole a Chinaman's soap, and used it lavishly; and, making their fingers do duty as tooth-brushes, they showed a purpose of cleanliness as well as of sport. It was really a charming picture— the water so clearly transparent; the beach shelving in smooth slopes of sand; the trees overarching the stream; beyond all, the Yosemite Fall swaying in silvery showers, and, in the foreground pool, these children of Nature playing, their tawny skins wet with water and glistening with all the beauty of animated bronze. After their bath, they favored me with their company. One pulled from its place of concealment a Jew's-harp, and my ears were regaled with "Shoo, Fly!"

This particular bend of the river proved to be a place of regular Indian resort; for, on another day, within a few yards of my chosen ground, there was an encampment of not less than half a dozen squaws, more young ones, and yet more dogs. A fire was burning on the slope under the cottonwood-trees, and in it were a number of stones of small size. A circular basin,, about three feet in diameter, and very shallow, had been carefully made in the fine sand, and into this acorn-flour was spread to the depth of three or four inches. The acorns are dried in the sun, hulled, and pounded between stones. By this rude process a very fine-looking, white flour is produced, but it is very bitter, and unfit for use until prepared. Conical baskets, of very fine osier, and filled with water, are made to stand securely by planting them in the sand. Into them hot stones are dropped, and in a few moments the strange spectacle is presented of a basket of water boiling violently. This scalding water is poured through cedar-boughs, held fan-like over the flour, until the sand-basin is full; it drains rapidly through; the process is repeated several times, until, on tasting, the flour proves to be sweet, the bitterness having all been leached away. The pasty mess is then scooped with the hands into one of the large baskets, mixed very thin with water, and into this gruel hot stones are dropped until it boils; it is stirred and cooked until about the consistency of mush, then it is considered good to eat. Up to this stage I had been intently watching, and seemed to interest the savages quite as much as they interested me. One of them, with a very limited stock of English, was evidently quite willing to use it for my benefit. I was invited to join them as they squatted about a large basket of *chemuck*, as they call it, which I did very readily. In addition to the chemuck, they had cooked, by the aid of hot stones, a very bitter weed, steeped it in water until it was tasteless, and that was now brought to add cheer to the festive scene. The youngest and most cleanly-looking squaw sat next to me, and made herself very agreeable by her aboriginal pleasantry and savage politeness. The old squaws were dirty beyond measure; they grinned as they ejaculated their gutturals, and seemed as willing to be agreeable as the younger ones. They honored me especially with a separate basket, holding maybe a quart of their acorn-gruel. I was desirous of tasting their preparation, even after having noted that all the water used was from the river in which the half-dozen or so of little Indians were making commendable efforts to get clean, marked by an unwillingness to duck and dive anywhere but in the very pools from which the cooking-supplies were drawn. But my nerves were strong and my purpose was stout to share the hospitality so kindly extended. The greens were put down by the chemuck, and the trial commenced by my red friend taking a quantity of the dripping greens, squeezing them dry in her hand, and offering them to me with pantomimic invitation to eat. With the quart of gruel in my lap and the squeezed greens in my hand, at the supreme moment I was any thing but hungry. They waited: I put the basket-bowl to my lips; they shook their heads, and their faces said that was not regular; my face asked what was the polite Indian manner. My kind friend promptly answered by first filling her mouth with greens, then dipping her four fingers into my gruel, ladling up a quantity, and then, with surprising quickness, transferring the half of her hand into her mouth. Further details are unnecessary. Up to this moment my stomach had

Yosemite Fall.

remained passive; now it rebelled. I nibbled timidly at
the greens, and dipped one finger into my chemuck.
A shout warned me that that would never do, and

again my red lady-friend set me an example, drawn from my private basket. I offered two, three fingers; they smiled derisively and shook their heads. The children and the dogs gathered around, and watched me with the wistfulness so peculiar to them. The situation was getting serious, so, with quick resolve and desperate energy, I plunged the half of my hand into the bowl; then, with a rapid twisting movement, tried to get it and the adhering gruel into my mouth. What a mess! Heart and stomach failed me, and my face told of complete discomfiture. With one guttural grunt and a peculiar grimness of expression, the entertainers turned to help themselves with all the spirit and appetite so wanting in their guest. All dipping into one dish, it was an exciting race. The youngsters ladled out their share, and the dogs were not behind, enjoying, as they did, the advantages of direct communication, without the drawback of hands. What was not eaten at once of the chemuck was again cooked until very thick, then dipped out into a small basket, and turned into the cold water of the river, in such manner as to harden and take the form of old-fashioned "turnovers." They really looked inviting as they lay, white and rounded, in a pool at the river-side. In this form they are fit for use for a number of days. Chemuck is flat and tasteless; there is no salt used in cooking but, to take its place, there is plenty of gritty sand. The sun went down behind Wa-haw-ka; the baskets and bread were gathered up, packed into the large cone baskets in which all loads are carried, strapped upon the backs of the oldest squaws, and they filed away, leaving their kitchen and banqueting-hall with no other trace of the day's work than the smouldering fire and the pits in the sand.

Hardly less nomadic or vagabond in character than the Indians were those rough fellows that found their way into the valley as mule-men, pedlers, and all those other nondescripts that are to be found hovering between the lines of civilization and the outer world of lawlessness. To such the grand excitement of the place was horse-racing, and the time invariably on Sunday. Any thing that looked like a horse might be a racer, and as great a tempest of excitement could be raised over a scrub of a mustang as though it were a thorough-bred. One Sunday morning I strolled to the upper end of the valley; a quiet like that of languor filled the air; the roar of the Yosemite Fall had died out, and now but a slender stream down the face of the cliff marked its place. In the hush I walked under the pine-trees, whose pendulous branches and long, tremulous needles vibrated into an Æolian melody upon the slightest provocation; a scarcely-perceptible breeze brought whispers, to be caught only by the attentive ear, that swelled through faultless crescendos into volumes of harmony, rich and deep, yet ever sounding strangely far away. From the shadows and music out to the sunlighted meadow was but a step. At the other extremity of the open space, four or five hundred yards away, was a group of men. Drawing

Merced Gorge.

nearer, it was plain to be seen that they were intent upon the preliminaries of a horse-race. There were Indians, Chinamen, Mexicans, negroes, and very dark-colored specimens of white men. There was a confusion of tongues, through which came the clear ring of clinking gold and silver coin, for all were betting—many of them their last dollar. Several horses were getting ready for the race; the favorites were a sorrel and a roan, or "blue horse;" all were very ordinary animals, and without the slightest training. There were no saddles; the riders, stripped of all superfluous clothing, bareheaded and barefooted, rode with only a sheepskin or bit of blanket under them; over the drawn-up knees and around the horse's body a surcingle was tightly drawn, binding horse and rider into one. Judges, starters, and umpires, were selected and positions taken. The word was given; the horses plunged, started, "bucked;" again they started; again the sorrel bucked. An unlimited amount of profanity expressed the impatience of the crowd. The "blue horse" was now largely the favorite.

"Now, boys, don't holler when the horses 's comin'—'cos you know the blue horse might fly the track—then whar's yer pile?"

"No! don't holler"— "we won't holler!" went up in one unanimous shout.

At last they came—a cloud of dust, rattling hoofs, and frantic riders plying their whips right and left over the struggling brutes under them; on they came; the squatting crowd sprang to their feet, and up went one simultaneous yell; on they came, the crowd capering, screaming, and "hollerin'," like so many madmen; all alike infected; the stoical Indian as well as the mercurial Mexican. "Now shet yer hollerin'," men of mercury, or, "whar's yer pile?" The "blue horse" led, and, in a cloud of dust, all dashed by. It was a whirlpool of excitement, the stake being the vortex. Round and round they went; shouts, laughter, and profanity—one wild, incoherent Babel—losers and winners alike indistinguishable. Their hot temperaments found the excitement they craved, and the losers were rewarded in its drunkenness. Yet another very different interest is to be found in the visitors who throng the valley. Probably not less than two thousand come and go between May and October of each year, and, without exaggeration, they may be said to represent every nation and class of people on the globe. For their accommodation there are three hotels, where excellent fare is to be had, all the difficulties of getting supplies being taken into consideration. An enterprising individual has opened a saloon, with a display of cut-glass and silver that is quite dazzling. A great mule, staggering under the slate-beds of a billiard-table, carried the heaviest load that has yet been taken into the valley; and plans were laid, that by this time may have been realized, for sledding a piano over the winter snow, to be added to the establishment. Here, too, is the telegraph-office, where a single telegraphic wire connects with the outer world. A fifth house has been built, or perched, fourteen hundred feet above the valley-bottom, on the small rock-level between the Vernal and Nevada Falls. The proprietors of these establishments hold them subject to leases granted by the Yosemite commissioners. The same authority also appoints a guardian of the valley, whose duty it is to see that the rules for the preservation of the trees and the prevention of wanton defacement are properly enforced.

The scenic effects of winter are described as wonderfully beautiful, the ice-forms about the falls being particularly interesting. No doubt in time it will be the fashion to make winter-excursions into the Yosemite, but for the present it is safe to advise that, if the visit cannot be made in May or June, it be deferred until another season, for later in the year, to the disappointment of losing some of the finest features in the scenery, are added the discomforts of heat, toil, and an all-pervading dust, that penetrates to the innermost recesses of one's baggage and being. The temperature of spring is delightful, but during summer the thermometer frequently stands as high as 96° and 98°, while on the plains it is away above 100°.

There are now no less than five trails over which a horse may get in or out of the valley: the Mariposa trail, passing Inspiration Point, and entering at the southern end; the Coulterville trail, that comes in at the same end, on the opposite side; a third trail, passing near Glacier Point, and entering at the foot of Sentinel Rock, about midway up the valley on its eastern side; a fourth one, passing through the Merced Gorge by the Vernal and Nevada Falls; and the fifth, through Indian Cañon, on the west side, north of Yosemite Fall. Over this last it is barely possible to get a horse, and it is very little used. On the Coulterville route travellers may ride in stages to the beginning of the descent, and at its foot may again take vehicles to the upper end of the valley—about four miles of level road—so reducing the horseback riding to but three miles. It is a mistake to think that the natural barriers—the walls surrounding—are impassable; there are many places where a bold climber could, without any great difficulty, surmount all obstacles.

The trail through Merced Gorge, after reaching the top of Nevada Fall, crosses the stream and the

Tenaya Cañon, from Glacier Point.

southern end of the Little or Upper Yosemite Valley.
This valley, more than two thousand feet above its
famous neighbor, is one of the many great granite

basins peculiar to this section of country. The bottom is a little more than three miles long, and is a pleasant succession of meadows and forests, through which flows the Merced River. The sides are not so much walls as smooth, bare slopes of seamless granite, ribboned with sienna brown bands from running water, and here and there breaking into those strange dome-forms so provocative of questions that as yet have received no answer.

Among our more extended excursions we planned one to this place, and, as we were to camp out for several days, our preparations were careful, and, on starting, our cavalcade was imposing. Five riders led; three pack-horses followed laden with hampers and blankets, each pack crowned with an inverted kettle or a broad frying-pan. After commencing the ascent, the way led through woods, close grown, and filled with a tangled undergrowth that, with all its rank vigor, was unable to overtop the great fragments of rock that strewed the forest. In places, the trail twisted from right to left in sharp zigzags, and was so exceedingly steep that the horse and rider upon the turn above seemed to be almost overhead. Within sight the river roared and tumbled in a series of cataracts. We left our horses under a great overhanging rock, in charge of the guide, to be taken up the trail to meet us farther on, while we climbed by a foot-path around the base of a magnificent cliff, and out, face to face with that beautiful sheet of falling water called the Vernal Fall. It is a curtain unbroken in its plunge of four hundred feet; on either side, the narrow gorge, drenched with spray and glimmering with rainbow-tints, is green with exuberant vegetable life. Climbing long ladders, we reached the top, to find a broad, basined rock and a lovely little lakelet sparkling in the sunlight. Farther on, we crossed a slender bridge, Wildcat Cataract flying underneath, just beyond which the little house already spoken of as between the Vernal and Nevada Falls found anchorage to the flat rock. Before us Nevada Fall came tumbling over a wall exceeding six hundred feet in height; to the right the Cap of Liberty, a singular form of granite, rose more than two thousand feet; all about were heights and depths, grand to look up to, terrible to look into. We had rejoined our guide and horses, and, passing through a clump of dark-looking firs that clustered at the foot of the Nevada Fall, we came out upon a slide of freshly-fractured, glistening granite that seemed impassable, but a way had been made, and up this avalanche of rock our horses betook themselves, climbing with wonderful pluck and sureness of foot. But one beast had shown a spirit of insubordination, so the guide had tied him close to a leader. At each angle of the zigzagging trail he would balk, refusing to follow; the other horse, keeping on regardless, pulled the obstinate creature into predicaments from which he could not extricate himself; then each pulled against the other, utterly indifferent as to consequences. In one of these contests the foothold of the leader gave way, and, in an instant, a confused mass of horse, an

General View of Yosemite,
from Summit of Cloud's Rest.

inextricable jumble of heads, legs, and tails, to say nothing of kettles and frying-pans, came bounding toward me; leaving the trail, the horses turned two or three somersaults among the broken rocks below, and then lay still, We clambered quickly down to them; they were not dead, did not even have any bones broken—their packs had saved them. One, lying wedged, with his feet in the air, received our first attention; ropes and straps were cut, and three of us undertook to roll the beast out of his position. No sooner did we get him to where he could use his legs, than he made one vehement effort, and we were tossed like children. I remember seeing a bald head, followed by a full complement of arms and legs, fly past me, as though projected from a catapult; the guide seemed to sink out of sight, and something, that struck very much after the manner of a trip-hammer, spread me on my back. In an instant we were upon our feet, to find that the horse had fallen upon the guide, who was lying under him pinned to the rock. Things now were really serious. Should the horse again struggle, the man under him would probably suffer fatal injury, so, another coming to the rescue, one sprung to the horse's head, holding it firmly down, while the other two, getting under the beast, lifted him bodily until the guide was able to drag himself out with nothing worse than a severely-sprained ankle and a bruised leg. It is not at all surprising that getting the horses on the trail proved much more difficult than their getting off. While the packs were being adjusted upon other horses, for these could barely hobble along, I made a sketch of the scene, looking down the gorge. In the distance is a glimpse of the western wall of the Yosemite. Nearer, on the left, is Glacier Point, rounding up to Sentinel Dome. The form to the right, in the middle of the picture, is a point called Crinoline, Sugar-Loaf, Verdant, and several other names. It is a spur from the shoulder of the Half-dome. The rock that forms the right of the sketch is a portion of the base of the Cap of Liberty. Resuming our way, we reached the upper valley late in the afternoon, and

found an ingeniously-constructed, evergreen brush-
house ready for us. It was short work to unpack and
unsaddle our horses, turn them loose, gather wood,
light a fire, and prepare our evening meal. During
preliminary proceedings the two ladies of our party
were engaged making gay and home-like the interior
of our hut. Bright-colored blankets were spread
with an eye critical to effect, and the heavy Mexican
saddles made capital lounges and pillows. A stroll in
twilight, until it deepened into moonlight, completed
the day. In spite of all our precautions, the first night
was really uncomfortable, owing to the cold; in the
morning a gray rime of frost covered every thing;
we were camping at an elevation greater than the
summit of Mount Washington.

From camp we made an excursion to the top of
Cloud's Rest, a point of view that surpasses all others
in its comprehensiveness, as it rises at least six thousand
feet above the Yosemite, or ten thousand above the sea.
Starting after an early breakfast, we rode for an hour
or two through open and scattered woods, climbing
rapidly. Not very far from the summit we entered a
remarkable grove of sugar-pines, through which ran
a small stream, where grass grew abundantly. We
took our horses to within a few hundred yards of the
summit, after cantering over a waste of disintegrating
granite, upon which stood, at wide intervals, strangely
grotesque pines, gaunt of limb and thick-bodied,
rigid and tendonous. Their branches were awry, as
if suddenly stayed while wrestling for life against the

storm, and their olive-brown verdure had no vital, sappy green to refresh the eye. Upon the blinding whiteness of the rock and sand were traced, in severe lines, shadows more wild and weird even than the real forms, and over all stretched a vault of "dusky violet," completing a picture almost without suggestion of our familiar world of beauty. Here we left our horses and climbed to the top, which proved to be a long, thin, wave-like crest of granite, very narrow and piled with loose blocks that looked so insecure that it required steady nerves to walk its length, which in places was not more than ten or twelve feet wide. On the east side the descent was a steep sweep for hundreds of feet; on the west it was thousands. It fell away in one unbroken surface of granite, at an angle of not less than 45°, with no obstacle to stay a falling body until it should reach the depths of Tenaya Cañon, at least a mile and a half distant. This slope is shown in the full-page illustration of Tenaya Cañon, where Cloud's Rest is the point just to the left of the Half-dome. It required some minutes to settle the nerves and look calmly about. To the north, over intervening cañons and gorges, the Sierra peaks rose grandly desolate, pale and delicately tinted with many tones, warm and cool, against the cloudless vacuum of the sky beyond, that, by contrast, wore a strangely sombre hue. Their shoulders were robed with snow and ice, and their flanks were grooved and scarred by glaciers long since extinct. Upon lower levels a sparse growth of evergreens hardly served to

Gorge of the Merced,
from Glacier Point Trail.

cover the naked appearance of the landscape, and bald spots of rock showed almost as white as the snow beyond. This peculiar appearance of sterility, and meagre, patchy forest-growth, characterizes all the surrounding country when seen from such a height. Turning from the Sierras, that were from three to five thousand feet above our level, we looked down six thousand feet into the Yosemite, whose peculiar, trough-like formation was readily recognizable, running almost at right angles to the regular trend of the mountains, and fully four thousand feet below the average level of the surrounding country. The familiar forms of the enclosing walls, and the green groves and meadows of the valley-floor upon which the Merced sparkled, could be plainly seen, but angles of rock hid each water-fall.

No one can really claim to have seen the best general view of the Yosemite until he has climbed Cloud's Rest. In the illustration the form on the left, in light, is the Half-dome, of which views from different positions are presented: first, in the opening picture; again, rising behind the figures in Horse-Racing; in the full-page engraving of Tenaya Cañon; from Glacier Point, and also from a point farther east, given on this page. Above it is Sentinel Dome, sloping down to Glacier Point; a small bit of Sentinel Rock projects just beyond. Farther away are the Cathedral Rocks and Spires. Opposed to them, on the right, is El Capitan. Immediately underneath, in the picture, is the North Dome, sweeping down to Washington Column, and separated from the Half-dome by Tenaya Cañon. The Yosemite Fall is to the right, and back of the North Dome. The Gorge of the Merced, and Nevada and Vernal Falls, are to the left, and back of the Half-dome. Bridal-veil Fall is back of the Cathedral Rocks, away in the distance. After a day or two we broke camp, and, by a new trail, over which we were the first to pass, made a *détour*, keeping along the upper edge of the Merced Gorge, crossing the Too-lulu-wack a few hundred yards above its fall, and thence to Glacier Point. This is one of the most interesting rides about the valley, presenting many grand and even startling views. From one point we could look down into what seemed a bottomless abyss, for it was impossible to see its greatest depth. Out of it came the roaring of distant waters and the lulling song of pine-tree forests. The Too-lulu-wack Fall was almost under us, and could not be seen; but on the opposite side were the Vernal and Nevada Falls and the many cataracts of the Merced that, unlike most of the other streams that enter the Yosemite, are very imposing all the year round. The Cap of Liberty rose prominently in the centre; back of that the upper Yosemite opened, and beyond all were the snow-capped High Sierras. In the engraving of this view, the peculiar rock-form and character of the upper valley walls or slopes have been quite lost. Passing on, we soon reached Glacier Point. At its northern end the Yosemite Valley divides in the form of a Y, Tenaya Cañon forming the left arm, and the Merced Gorge the right. Again, the Merced Gorge is divided like a T, the Merced entering on the left, the Too-lulu-wack on the right. Glacier Point is a spur of rock or mountain jutting out on the west or right-hand side of the valley, where it divides. From its terraced summit we looked down thirty-two hundred feet to the meadows at our very feet. Few can gaze into such a depth without a shudder. Directly opposite, on the other side, perhaps a mile and a half away, the Yosemite Fall came down half a mile in three leaps, its truly graceful proportions seen to greater advantage than from any other point. To the right, or north, we looked up Tenaya Cañon, its narrow floor beautiful

Half-dome.

with tall pines that almost hid its one jewel, Mirror Lake; but with walls grim and vast that swept on the right up five thousand feet to the grand, dominating form of the valley, the Half-dome. The bald slope and crest of Cloud's Rest towered beyond, and back of all the Sierras lifted their peaks, as yet untrodden by the foot of man. There can be but few places where so much of the terrible and the beautiful are at once combined.

From Glacier Point a trail leads to the summit of Sentinel Dome. Upon this height we spent an hour or more, enjoying already familiar features as viewed from a new stand-point. The ride thence to Paregoy's, distant about six miles, was through heavy forest. From Paregoy's we, brothers of the brush, returned to our old quarters in the valley, and worked hard for two months to bring away some limned shadow, however faint, of the wonders about us. At last our work was done, and our traps were packed for departure. Familiar with horses, pack-mules, and trails, we were independent of guides. The valley was filled with morning shadows when we started on our way. I led, dragging after me an extremely recusant pack-mule, that was pricked into conformity by G——, who followed, armed with a formidable stick, at least six feet long. Between our horses, the mule, and "last looks," much time was consumed, but Paregoy's was reached before one o'clock, and the late afternoon was spent trying to get a study of evening tints over the Sierras. The colorless granite is singularly responsive to certain atmospheric effects. Against a background of storm-cloud their forms stand wan and ghost-like; in the blinding glare of the mid-day sun they faint, almost indistinguishable; and, at sunset, they glow with a ruddy light, that is slowly extinguished by the upcreeping shadows of night, until the highest point flames for one moment, then dies, ashy pale, under the glory that is lifted to the sky above. Then the cold moon tips with silver those giant, sleeping forms, and by its growing light I cleared my palette, and closed the box upon my last study of the Yosemite and Sierras.